Original title:
Starlit Pines

Copyright © 2024 Swan Charm
All rights reserved.

Author: Olivia Oja
ISBN HARDBACK: 978-9916-79-825-6
ISBN PAPERBACK: 978-9916-79-826-3
ISBN EBOOK: 978-9916-79-827-0

The Tranquility of Night's Luminous Crown

In the velvet sky so wide,
The moon casts its gentle light,
A crown of stars that softly bide,
Whispers secrets of the night.

Clouds drift like dreams in flight,
While shadows dance on the ground,
A calm that feels so right,
In this silent, sacred sound.

The world holds its breath so still,
As time slows to a gentle sigh,
Every heart begins to fill,
With the lullaby of the sky.

Crickets serenade the dusk,
Nature's symphony unfolds,
In this peace, we find our trust,
In stories night silently holds.

Each star a shimmering thought,
A wish upon a distant gleam,
In the tranquility sought,
We find a place to dream.

Murmurs of Stars in the Cascading Boughs

Underneath the whispering trees,
Stars peek through leaves so green,
They brush against the evening breeze,
In a dance so serene.

Branches sway with tales untold,
With each rustle, a secret shared,
In the darkness, wonders unfold,
By gentle hands, the night is prepared.

Softly glows the silver light,
As shadows play upon the ground,
A melody of pure delight,
In the night, our dreams are found.

The sky hums a lullaby,
While crickets join in the song,
Beneath the watchful night so high,
We feel that we belong.

Each glimmer tells a story neat,
Of distant worlds yet to explore,
In this realm, our hearts entreat,
The murmurs of stars we adore.

Where Nebulas Meet Quiet Pines

In twilight's hush, the stars ignite,
Whispers dance in the cool night.
Pines stand tall, guardians of dreams,
Under skies where stardust gleams.

Fleeting shadows, soft and shy,
Leave their secrets as they fly.
Nebulas swirl in colors bright,
Painting stories in the night.

A breeze carries a fragrant song,
Nature's voice, gentle and strong.
Crickets chirp in rhythmic grace,
In this tranquil, sacred space.

The cool earth cradles weary hearts,
As silent magic slowly starts.
Unity found in night's embrace,
Where the cosmos reveals its face.

Here we linger, lost in time,
In the rhythm of nature's rhyme.
Each moment glows with pure delight,
Where nebulas meet the quiet night.

Echoes of the Moonlit Grove

Beneath the moon's soft, silver glow,
The ancient trees stand row by row.
Whispers drift on balmy air,
Stories linger, rich and rare.

The brook sings low, a calming tune,
Freed from the grasp of the afternoon.
Ghostly shadows weave and sway,
As twilight beckons the end of day.

Stars peek through the canopy wide,
Dancing lights that glide and hide.
Each rustle tells a tale untold,
Of countless nights both young and old.

In the grove where silence reigns,
Echoes linger, sweet refrains.
Hearts converse with the breeze,
In this realm of ancient trees.

A moment held, so precious, bright,
In shadows cast by gentle light.
Forever cradled in night's glove,
The echoes of the moonlit grove.

Glowing Reflections Beneath the Branches

Inforest depths, where light cascades,
Shadows dance in sun-kissed glades.
Leaves shimmer with a golden hue,
As sunlight spills through branches true.

Meandering paths of ancient lore,
Lead to places we adore.
Rippling streams mirror the sky,
Where thoughts can linger, drift and sigh.

Beneath the green's protective screen,
Lost in worlds that once have been.
Nature speaks in whispers soft,
Inviting dreams to rise aloft.

A tapestry of life unfolds,
In painted hues, both bright and bold.
Every moment, a gentle sigh,
In the forest's arms, we fly.

Reflections glow, a tranquil art,
Binding nature to the heart.
Beneath the branches, peace will grow,
In glowing whispers, softly flow.

Serenity Among the Glimmering Foliage

In emerald realms where stillness reigns,
Serenity flows through gentle veins.
Twilight drapes in softest hues,
A sacred haven for hearts to choose.

Leaves shimmer with a lustrous sheen,
In the light where wonders glean.
Every rustle speaks of calm,
Nature's heartbeat, a gentle psalm.

Cool breezes weave through boughs up high,
Carrying secrets, low and nigh.
Here, time reverberates slow,
In this refuge, tranquility flows.

Among the trees, a soft embrace,
Finding solace in every space.
Each leaf a friend, each branch a guide,
In shimmering foliage, dreams abide.

As evening falls, the stars appear,
A necklace strung, both far and near.
In this gentle, glowing light,
Serenity reigns through the night.

The Constellation of Stillness

In twilight's glow, shadows dance,
Whispers drift on a quiet chance.
Stars above in a velvet night,
Silent secrets holding light.

The air is thick with dreams untold,
Time stands still, a moment bold.
Crickets sing a lullaby,
As the world breathes out a sigh.

Beneath the vast, unending sky,
Thoughts take flight, like birds they fly.
Each twinkle, a memory profound,
In stillness, solace can be found.

Nature wraps in its gentle arms,
With each heartbeat, the night disarms.
The universe hums a soothing tune,
As stillness reigns beneath the moon.

Embrace the quiet, let it swell,
In these depths, we know so well.
The constellation of pure grace,
In stillness, find your rightful place.

Forests of Ethereal Beauty

In forests deep where shadows play,
The sunbeams pierce the leafy fray.
Soft whispers echo through the trees,
As nature basks in soft, warm breeze.

Moss carpets ground with emerald hue,
A tapestry of life anew.
Branches weave a natural dome,
In this haven, we are home.

Wildflowers sprinkle the forest floor,
With colors bright, they softly implore.
Sweet scents waft and interlace,
In this beauty, we find our grace.

Birdsongs harmonize through the air,
Each note a promise, light as prayer.
In this realm of tranquil delight,
Magic glimmers in the light.

Forests whisper ancient tales,
Of time and life that never fails.
In ethereal beauty, we remain,
Connected to the earth's refrain.

Bedtime Stories Among Pine Needles

Beneath the boughs where shadows sleep,
In a cradle of pine, dreams run deep.
Stories whisper through the night,
Guiding hearts with gentle light.

The moon drapes silver on the ground,
While pinecones rest, in silence found.
Rustling leaves share secrets rare,
As we breathe in the cool night air.

Tales of stars and far-off lands,
Adventures born from whispered plans.
With every breath, a world unfolds,
In this magic, life beholds.

Crickets sing a soft refrain,
While the night wraps us in its chain.
Among the needles, dreams take flight,
Sleeping soundly, till morning light.

In these woods, hearts find their peace,
Where bedtime stories never cease.
Among the pines, we drift away,
To the land of dreams where we sway.

The Allure of Celestial Canopies

In midnight hues of deep indigo,
The universe reveals its glow.
Galaxies swirl in endless grace,
Painting dreams in boundless space.

Among these vast celestial scenes,
Stardust glimmers like silver means.
Constellations draw our gaze,
In their magic, we are ablaze.

The allure of the skies above,
Whispers tales of hope and love.
Stars acknowledge, twinkling bright,
Guiding souls through the night.

Underneath this cosmic veil,
We find comfort in every tale.
A dance of light, a glimpse of fate,
Celestial canopies captivate.

In every shimmer, a wish is born,
Like gentle dewdrops on the lawn.
In this vastness, we belong,
Entranced by the universe's song.

Twilight's Kiss on the Needles

Beneath the pine's tall sway, the shadows play,
The whispering winds, they softly sway.
Dewdrops cling like jewels, pure and bright,
As day descends into the quiet night.

The stars emerge, a glimmering lace,
In nature's arms, we find our place.
The twilight air, a cool embrace,
Every heartbeat, a peaceful trace.

Moonlight dances on the forest floor,
An echoing tune, forevermore.
The needles sigh with stories untold,
As dreams take flight, both brave and bold.

In every rustle, a note of grace,
A symphony played in this sacred space.
We linger longer where shadows blend,
In twilight's kiss, our hearts we send.

Song of the Silvered World

When night unfolds her silken cloak,
The silvered streams begin to soak.
With every ripple, a secret shared,
In quiet moments, our hearts laid bare.

The moon hums soft with golden gleam,
Awakens all within the dream.
A melody kissed by the autumn breeze,
Calls to the spirits of ancient trees.

Through shadows deep and whispers light,
The song of stars ignites the night.
Each note a spark, each breath a sigh,
In the tender dark, our dreams can fly.

Let the echoes of the past be known,
In silver whispers, we find our home.
Together we sing, in love's embrace,
A timeless dance, an endless grace.

Chasing Stardust Among the Boughs

Underneath the canopy wide,
We chase the stardust, side by side.
In every flicker, a world anew,
Among the leaves, our spirits grew.

The night is young, our laughter rings,
As fireflies waltz on gossamer wings.
We weave our dreams in paths of light,
Together lost in this magical night.

Whispers of nature, sweet and clear,
As constellations draw us near.
We gather wishes from every star,
Mapping our future, no dream too far.

With each heartbeat, the universe sings,
Chasing stardust, we find our wings.
Beneath the boughs, forever we'll stay,
In this enchanted night, come what may.

Enchanted by the Cosmic Night

The cosmos spreads in hues so deep,
Awakens dreams we dare to keep.
Galaxies swirl in a vibrant dance,
Inviting us to take a chance.

The rhythm of the stars, so clear,
In every heartbeat, magic near.
We trace the paths where comets glide,
In the ocean of night, we will confide.

Nebulas bloom in colors bright,
Painting stories across the night.
Each moment's spark, a timeless pledge,
As we stand on this cosmic edge.

Eclipsed in wonder, our souls ignite,
Enchanted by the cosmic night.
With every breath, the universe calls,
In its embrace, our spirit enthralls.

The Symphony of Night's Embrace

Whispers weave through shadows bright,
Stars alight in velvet night.
Moonbeams dance on silken streams,
Crickets chirp in soft moonbeams.

A breeze carries secrets near,
Rustling leaves, the night draws near.
Fireflies flicker, tales unfold,
Nature's magic, pure and bold.

The world is hushed in sweet delight,
As dreams take flight in soft twilight.
Hearts entwined beneath the sky,
Lost in moments, you and I.

Echoes linger, time will pause,
In night's symphony, we find cause.
To cherish every fleeting glance,
Together in this perfect dance.

Enchanted Spaces of the Celestial Woods

Among the trees where shadows play,
Whispers of magic drift away.
Golden leaves in sunlight's beam,
Nature's wonders, like a dream.

Veils of mist in dawn's embrace,
Hidden paths in timeless space.
Gentle streams with laughter flow,
Secrets of the woods will show.

Wildflowers bloom in colors rare,
Breathing life through fragrant air.
Forest spirits, soft as sighs,
Guard the dreams beneath the skies.

Time stirs softly, moments linger,
In each heart, a gentle finger.
Guiding souls through tranquil days,
In enchanted woods, we play.

Celestial Flames Among Nature's Guardians

In twilight's glow, the embers spark,
A fiery dance ignites the dark.
Ancient trees stand tall and wise,
Guardians watching starry skies.

Through the branches, flames take flight,
Painting dreams with vibrant light.
A symphony of warmth and glow,
Nature's beauty, a sacred show.

Each flicker holds a story old,
Of whispered secrets, dreams untold.
The heart of earth, the fire's thread,
Binding life with warmth we spread.

Celestial flames, they softly weave,
In every heart, a chance to believe.
For in the night, we find our place,
Among the guardians, we embrace.

Twilight Wonders Hidden Among the Fir

Beneath the fir, where shadows play,
Twilight wonders beckon sway.
A canvas painted, dusk's embrace,
Nature's whispers find their space.

Softly rustling, branches sigh,
Secrets linger, drifting high.
Mossy carpets, emerald dreams,
Closer to the starlit beams.

In hidden corners, stories linger,
Midnight blooms with gentle finger.
Fireflies weave a dance so bright,
In the heart of soft twilight.

Embraced by peace, the world feels near,
Silent echoes, memories clear.
Among the fir, we find our way,
In twilight wonders, here to stay.

Luminescence in the Boughs

A glow wakes softly in the trees,
Casting shadows, dancing leaves.
Whispers of light, in emerald play,
Nature's secrets held at bay.

Moonlit paths weave tales untold,
Through branches bent, and spirits bold.
Each flicker, a step in the dark,
A symphony where echoes spark.

Crickets sing their nightly tune,
Beneath the watch of a silver moon.
As fireflies weave their golden lace,
In this enchanted, sacred space.

Time drifts gently, a feathered sigh,
Where magic blurs and dreams can fly.
Among the boughs, soft wonders dwell,
A whispered world we know so well.

From dusk to dawn, we learn to see,
The quiet songs of what can be.
In luminescence, hope will rise,
Illuminated beneath the skies.

Dance of the Cosmic Fir

Stars cascade, like rain from night,
In the bosom of a fir, so bright.
Branches stretch in cosmic grace,
While shadows twirl in a breathless space.

Celestial whispers hum and glide,
As galaxies spin, in twinkling pride.
The earth beneath holds its breath tight,
In the embrace of cosmic light.

Each needle shines with ancient lore,
Tales of light from the heavens' core.
A dance unfolds beneath the sky,
In silence, where the stardust lies.

Echoes call from the endless deep,
Awakening dreams from celestial sleep.
With every sway, the universe sighs,
In the magic of the dark blue skies.

Beneath the fir, we lose our way,
In the rhythm of night and day.
A cosmic dance forever spun,
In the heart of each setting sun.

Dreams Held by Whispering Glades

In glades where whispers weave their song,
Dreams unfurl where hearts belong.
Petals softly kiss the ground,
In secret spaces, lost yet found.

Sunlight dapples through green lace,
Turning shadows into grace.
Each breath a tale of yesteryear,
In gentle breezes, memories near.

Winding paths through wildflower blooms,
Breathe life amidst nature's tunes.
In the hush, where time stands still,
Dreams awaken with tranquil thrill.

Beneath the trees, we close our eyes,
To hear the world's soft lullabies.
These glades hold secrets, journeys vast,
In the whispering winds of the past.

With every rustle, a story is spun,
In twilight's glow, the night's begun.
Dreams held softly, in nature's hands,
Calling us to enchanted lands.

Lightfall Among Woodland Shadows

Golden rays break through the trees,
Kissing leaves in a gentle breeze.
Shadows dance upon the ground,
As whispers of light abound.

The forest breathes a sigh of relief,
Embracing both joy and grief.
Each beam a thread in nature's seam,
Weaving together a timeless dream.

Among the ferns, secrets lay,
In lightfall's warm, embracing sway.
Mossy carpets cradle the dawn,
Where night's magic has nearly withdrawn.

In quietude, the heart will find,
A solace deep, a bond entwined.
With every flicker, shadows recede,
In woodland whispers, peace we breed.

As daylight wanes, the stars ignite,
Echoes of dusk confound the night.
In the transition, life's moments blend,
A dance of shadows that never end.

Echoes in the Forest of Stars

Whispers in the cool night air,
Beneath a sky of glittering gems,
Each star a tale of ancient care,
In silent woods, the magic stems.

Moonlight dances on the leaves,
Casting shadows, soft and grand,
Nature's sigh, the heart it weaves,
In this enchanted, timeless land.

The river sings of dreams untold,
As fireflies twinkle, break the dark,
In sacred spaces, fears unfold,
Here, magic ignites a spark.

Branches cradle the cosmic light,
While creatures roam beneath the haze,
Stars above, a wondrous sight,
In the night's soft, tender ways.

Luminous Dreams Beneath the Pines

Underneath the pines, I lay,
Softly dreaming, mind takes flight,
Moonbeams guiding, bright as day,
Wrapped in serenity of night.

Swaying boughs sing lullabies,
Gentle rustle, nature's breath,
In this peace my spirit flies,
Finding solace, escaping death.

Stars whisper secrets, oh so near,
Each twinkle holds a fleeting wish,
A tapestry of dreams appear,
Nurtured deep by the night's own dish.

Into slumber, I drift away,
With pine-scent dreams, a fragrant balm,
Tomorrow brings a brand new day,
For now, I rest in nature's calm.

Nightfall's Embrace in the Treetops

As twilight wraps the tree's embrace,
Shadows brush the forest floor,
Quiet moments, a tranquil space,
Where nature whispers evermore.

The call of owls breaks the night,
As stars peek through the leafy veil,
In the hush, there's pure delight,
In dreams where spirit does not fail.

Branches sway, the night wind sings,
A melody that soars and flies,
To the heart of all living things,
Underneath the velvet skies.

Laughter lingers in the dark,
As shadows dance and spirits play,
In the treetops, life leaves its mark,
A night woven in the stars' ballet.

Secrets in the Twilight Woods

Hidden paths where whispers dwell,
Twilight softens every hue,
In the woods, there's magic's spell,
Drawing secrets old and new.

Leaves converse in muted tones,
Every rustle tells a tale,
Of dreams and wishes, ancient moans,
In this sacred, leafy trail.

Glowing softly, fireflies blink,
Guiding footsteps through the night,
Nature's wonders urge me to think,
Of all the mysteries in sight.

In the twilight, time stands still,
Encased in shadows, deep and wide,
With each heartbeat, my heart will fill,
As nature's wonders gently bide.

The Constellation of Whispering Trees

Beneath the stars, they softly sway,
In whispers loud, the night holds play.
Their branches dance with gentle grace,
A tranquil song in nature's space.

The moonlight weaves through leaves so bright,
Casting shadows, a wondrous sight.
Each rustle tells a tale untold,
Of secrets kept and dreams of old.

Their roots entwined beneath the ground,
In silent strength, their peace is found.
Together they stand, a timeless band,
In harmony, they softly stand.

As breezes lift the leaves in flight,
The trees converse throughout the night.
With every sigh and every breeze,
They weave the dreams of whispering trees.

In stillness lies their sacred truth,
A dance of age, a song of youth.
In every rustle, every plea,
The constellation of whispering trees.

Glowing Horizons Beyond the Pines

At dusk the glow begins to rise,
A canvas painted 'cross the skies.
The pines stand tall, a darkened line,
Against the hues where day aligns.

The sunset spills its fiery threads,
Where golden light on dark earth spreads.
Beyond the pines, the dreams ignite,
And dance upon the edge of night.

A whisper calls from heights above,
The glowing gold like warmest love.
Each shadow lengthens, day's refrain,
In twilight's hold, we break the chain.

The colors fade, but not the hope,
Through dusky paths, our spirits cope.
From every branch, a tale it twines,
Of glowing horizons beyond the pines.

And as the stars emerge for play,
We leave our burdens, come what may.
In every glow, a promise shines,
To guide us home beyond the pines.

Nature's Ballet Under Star-Studded Skies

In twilight's grasp, the world awakes,
With every breeze, the night heart breaks.
The trees start swaying, grace at sea,
In nature's ballet, wild and free.

The stars above twinkle so bright,
They guide the dance through velvet night.
With every step in shadows cast,
They twirl and leap, time's frame surpassed.

The moon, a spotlight on the stage,
Illuminates the vibrant page.
Every leaf in motion's thrill,
A symphony, a whisper's will.

The gentle hush of night descends,
As all around the beauty blends.
Alive with magic, soft and shy,
Nature's ballet beneath the sky.

With every swirl, a moment caught,
The earth and night in harmony sought.
In starlit grace, our hearts comply,
To nature's ballet, no goodbye.

Illuminated Solitude in the Silent Woods

In silent woods, the shadows play,
With soft embrace at end of day.
Each step whispers on the floor,
As nature cradles and restores.

The trees stand guard, their secrets kept,
In tranquil shades where dreams have crept.
Illuminated by the moon,
The silence sings a gentle tune.

A pathway glimmers, soft and light,
Where solitude meets the calm of night.
With every breath, a world awakes,
In tender stillness, kindness breaks.

The fireflies dance in endless sway,
Their glowing paths a wild ballet.
In unity, they paint the dark,
A constellation, love's own spark.

In solitude, we find our peace,
In woods where all our worries cease.
Amidst the silence, hearts are stirred,
Illuminated solitude, unblurred.

Luminescent Spirits in Verdant Whispers

In the night, the shadows play,
Whispers soft where fairies stay.
Greens and gold in silent grace,
Nature's dance, a fond embrace.

Stars above, they twinkle bright,
Casting dreams in silver light.
In the air, a magic hum,
Lifetimes lost in twilight's drum.

Trees adorned with glowing sighs,
Mysteries that never dies.
Underneath their boughs so wide,
Spirits flourish, hearts abide.

Crickets chirp amidst the night,
Guiding souls with sweet delight.
Moonlit paths, a glowing stream,
Nature weaves a precious dream.

In the hush of leafy green,
Life unfolds, serene, unseen.
Luminescent spirits glide,
Through the whispers, they confide.

When Time Stands Still Among the Trees

In their shade, the moments freeze,
Nature speaks among the trees.
Leaves like pages softly turn,
Lessons of the past they learn.

Boughs embrace, a woven tale,
Caught in wind, a fleeting sail.
Echoes of a whispered breeze,
In the silence, hearts find ease.

Sunlight drips like honey sweet,
At the roots, the earth's heartbeat.
Here we pause, a sigh on lips,
In this pause, the world then slips.

Every shadow a soft guide,
Time's embrace, we can't divide.
Among the trunks where dreams entwine,
We find solace, thin with time.

Stillness reigns as night descends,
In the whisper, all transcends.
Stars emerge, secrets unfurl,
Dreams awaken, night's sweet pearl.

Glowing Echoes in Time's Embrace

Through the twilight, shadows bloom,
Glowing echoes break the gloom.
Mystic rivers whisper low,
Time moves with a gentle flow.

Flickering lights, the stars align,
In their glow, the worlds combine.
Every heartbeat resonates,
With the magic that awaits.

A tapestry of light and sound,
In this moment, we are found.
Echoes weave a sweet refrain,
Holding memories, joy and pain.

As dawn approaches, whispers fade,
Time's embrace, a promise made.
Yet the glow shall ever stay,
In our hearts, it lights the way.

In the silence, truths align,
Glowing echoes, so divine.
Through the years, they will inspire,
Fanning thoughts like gentle fire.

Visual Symphony of the Midnight Grove

In the midnight, colors blend,
Nature's art, our hearts transcend.
Underneath the velvet sky,
Harmony in shadows high.

Branches sway like conductor's hands,
Guiding dreams in vibrant bands.
Notes of night, they softly cling,
To the symphony of spring.

Whispers dance on zephyr's wing,
Nature's chorus starts to sing.
Moonbeams glance on painted leaves,
Stories shared, the heart believes.

Crickets play a wild refrain,
Setting free our deepest pain.
Every star a note in flight,
Crafting beauty in the night.

In this grove, all senses sway,
Lost in joy, we drift away.
Visual symphony unfolds,
As the midnight's magic holds.

Revelations in Twilight Sanctuaries

In shadows deep where secrets lie,
Whispers breathe a silent sigh.
The twilight hues softly blend,
As day relinquishes its end.

Stars awaken, their stories told,
In golden threads of dreams unfold.
A sanctuary wrapped in night,
Where wonders bloom in muted light.

The breeze carries a haunting tune,
Caressing leaves beneath the moon.
Each rustle sings of time's embrace,
In this sacred, tranquil place.

With every glance, the heart ignites,
As visions dance in tranquil flights.
A tapestry of fate we weave,
In twilight's grasp, we dare believe.

Emerging truths like fireflies gleam,
Illuminating every dream.
The darkness hums its soulful art,
Unveiling worlds within the heart.

Celestial Tales Among Cedar Branches

Beneath the boughs where legends sleep,
Ancient stories gently creep.
The cedars whisper, tall and grand,
Of distant stars, woven by hand.

Moonlight dapples on the ground,
A symphony of nature's sound.
In this grove, the air does sing,
Of time's embrace and every spring.

Each branch a tale, each leaf a song,
In harmony, where dreams belong.
A canopy of magic sways,
Entwined in night's enchanting haze.

Celestial bodies glow so bright,
Guiding souls through endless night.
Among the cedar's guarding grace,
We find our truth, our sacred space.

With every heartbeat, bonds are made,
In shadows stretched where sunlight played.
The universe bids us to explore,
And for each tale, we yearn for more.

Whispers of Light Through Leafy Halls

In leafy halls where sunlight streams,
Gentle whispers weave their dreams.
Nature's choir sings in delight,
A tapestry of purest light.

Each ray dances, a fleeting guest,
Awakening life from gentle rest.
Through emerald canopies they thread,
Illuminating paths ahead.

The rustling leaves share ancient lore,
Of seasons past and life's great score.
In every corner, shadows play,
As daylight bids the dark away.

A melody flows through fragile trees,
As whispers ride upon the breeze.
Awash in light, the spirit soars,
Echoing through these sacred doors.

In nature's arms, all hearts align,
With every breath, we intertwine.
These leafy halls, a refuge found,
In whispers of light, our souls unbound.

Night's Veil Over Timeless Roots

As night descends with velvet grace,
A soft embrace for every place.
Timeless roots in slumber deep,
Guard secrets that we long to keep.

Beneath the stars, the earth does sigh,
In whispered tones, both low and high.
Night unfurls its velvet cloak,
A gentle hush, like stories woke.

Through tangled vines, the shadows weave,
In darkness, we learn how to believe.
Each pulse of light a guiding hand,
For wandering souls across the land.

With wisdom grown from years gone by,
The roots connect, and spirits fly.
In every breath, the past recalls,
The promise held as night enthralls.

A symphony of cosmic rhyme,
Reminds us of the dance with time.
In night's embrace, we find our way,
As voices blend and fade away.

Enchanted Dialogue with the Night.

Beneath the stars we softly tread,
Voices carried where dreams are fed.
The night sings sweet in silken tones,
A melody of ancient stones.

Whispers rustle through the leaves,
In twilight's grasp, each heart believes.
The moon winks down with silver grace,
Illuminating this sacred space.

Time slips by on gossamer wings,
As every shadow gently clings.
With every breath, the night invites,
A dance beneath the jeweled lights.

Boundless the stories in the dark,
Echoes left by a fleeting spark.
We share our thoughts in hushed delight,
In this enchanted, starry night.

Embrace the magic, oh, so rare,
In whispered secrets, we declare.
Together here, no fear or fright,
Lost in the embrace of the night.

Whispers of the Night Canopy

Stars peek through a leafy shroud,
Nightingales sing soft and loud.
In the silence, secrets flow,
Underneath the moon's soft glow.

Branches sway with gentle grace,
Holding time in this sacred place.
The gentle breeze a chorus makes,
While slumbering earth in stillness wakes.

A tapestry of dreams unfolds,
In whispers shared, our hopes are told.
In every rustle, a heart's refrain,
Echoes linger, sweet like rain.

Above, the cosmos paints its art,
With constellations, we take part.
A canopy of wonder bright,
Welcomes us into the night.

Embrace the tales known by the stars,
As night embraces with gentle bars.
From dusk till dawn, time stands still,
In whispers soft, our souls we fill.

Moonlight Dances Among the Evergreens

Beneath the boughs, the shadows play,
As moonlight weaves through night and day.
The laughter of the leaves does rise,
In this enchanted paradise.

Each glimmer beckons with a sigh,
As echoes of the night float by.
The cedar stands in quiet grace,
A guardian of this sacred place.

Dancing beams on silver moss,
A gentle touch, no need for gloss.
In this serene and timeless hour,
Nature blooms with every flower.

Footsteps light, they softly tread,
Among the trees, where dreams are bred.
The moon's embrace, a tender guide,
While shadows linger, side by side.

Forever woven, night's embrace,
In every heart, a sacred space.
With every dance under stars so bright,
We lose ourselves in the soothing night.

Shadows of the Celestial Grove

In twilight's arms, the shadows rest,
Among the trees, the heart feels blessed.
Whispering secrets, spirits glide,
In the grove where mysteries hide.

Celestial wonders dance and twirl,
As the soft winds begin to swirl.
The night unveils her silver crown,
With every heartbeat, love is found.

In the quiet, a sigh takes flight,
Under the glow of stars so bright.
Each moment holds a story rare,
Woven through the moonlit air.

The earth breathes tales of ancient lore,
Echoing in each open door.
In shadows, dreams begin to form,
In this enchanted night, so warm.

Together here, we watch the skies,
As constellations rise and rise.
Within the grove, where spirits rove,
We find ourselves in the celestial grove.

Nature's Lanterns in the Forest Depths

In the heart of trees so tall,
Fireflies dance, a glowing thrall.
Whispers float on gentle breeze,
Nature's magic, hearts at ease.

Moonlight spills on leaves of green,
Casting shadows, softly seen.
Stars above, a twinkling flow,
Guide the way where wild things go.

Mossy carpets underfoot,
Secrets lie where roots take root.
A symphony of nightingale,
Nature's song, a sweet exhale.

Breezes carry scents so sweet,
In this realm, reflections meet.
Every creature finds a place,
Woven tight in nature's grace.

Through the trees, the lanterns glow,
Illuminating paths we know.
In the stillness, time stands still,
Nature speaks, and hearts will thrill.

Beneath a Veil of Glowing Orbs

Beneath the night where dreams unfold,
Orbs of light, a tale retold.
Glimmers dancing on the lake,
Whispers linger, memories wake.

Cerulean skies, the stars ignite,
Nature's artistry in flight.
Every wave a tale to share,
Glowing orbs in moonlit air.

Rippling waters, soft and clear,
Underneath, secrets disappear.
Echoes of the past arise,
Bathed in silver, night's reprise.

In the quiet, mysteries breathe,
As the cosmos starts to weave.
Eternal dance of light and shade,
In this moment, dreams are made.

Hearts aligned with nature's flow,
Beneath the veil, we truly know.
Lost in beauty, we reside,
In the night, we turn the tide.

Harmony of Shadows and Shimmering Lights

Beneath the trees, where shadows lay,
Shimmering lights begin to play.
A twilight hush, the world takes pause,
Nature's harmony, a silent cause.

Each flicker tells a story bright,
Guiding lost souls through the night.
Under boughs where secrets breathe,
Magic dances, webs we weave.

Crickets chirp in rhythmic tune,
Stars emerge, a silver boon.
Murmurs flow like rivers wide,
In gentle arcs, time does abide.

Leaves rustle, a soft refrain,
In this realm, love knows no pain.
Shadows stretch, embracing light,
A ballet of day and night.

Harmony in every vein,
Nature speaks, amidst the rain.
Whispers linger, dreams take flight,
In shadows deep and shimmering light.

Ethereal Reflections on Ancient Roots

Worn and wise, the ancient trees,
Whisper tales upon the breeze.
Roots entwined with history,
Reflections fade, like mystery.

Moonlight kisses every knoll,
Illuminating nature's soul.
In the stillness, spirits leap,
Lost in time where shadows sleep.

Ferns unfurl in quiet grace,
Each a guardian of this place.
Ethereal glow, a gentle guide,
Through the whispers, we confide.

In the depths, where dreams entwine,
Ancient roots and hearts align.
A tapestry of dusk and dawn,
In nature's arms, we wander on.

Here, the past and now collide,
In reflections where we bide.
Eternal beauty, ever near,
In every heartbeat, we draw near.

A Lullaby of Lights and Shadows

In the hush of evening glow,
Shadows dance with a gentle flow.
Stars above begin to gleam,
Cradled in a whispered dream.

Moonlight weaves through boughs so deep,
Softly calling all to sleep.
Gentle breeze sings lullabies,
As the world in silence lies.

Crickets chirp their sweet refrain,
In the coolness, joy and pain.
Nature cradles every sigh,
Till the dawn draws nigh.

Let the darkness hold you tight,
In the tender arms of night.
Rest your head and close your eyes,
While the silent magic flies.

Dreams take flight on silver beams,
Flowing softly like our dreams.
In this peace, we find our way,
Guided gently by the gray.

Footsteps in the Cosmic Wilderness

Beneath the vast celestial sea,
Footsteps wander, ever free.
Galaxies twirl in a cosmic dance,
While stars ignite a daring chance.

Infinite paths stretch and bend,
To horizons where stars transcend.
Whispers of planets call us near,
In this wildness, we lose all fear.

Nebulas bloom with colors bright,
Painting dreams that softly ignite.
Galactic winds carry our cries,
As we trace the ancient skies.

With every stride, we touch the vast,
Wonders of the night's contrast.
The universe sings a sweet refrain,
In this wilderness, we gain.

Let the cosmos guide your way,
Amidst the stardust, souls at play.
In this sacred realm we roam,
Every heartbeat feels like home.

Echoes of Light in Timeless Woods

In the woods where shadows dwell,
Softly stirring, a whispered spell.
Sunbeams filter through the leaves,
Carving paths where the heart believes.

Echoes linger, tales unfold,
Of ancient spirits, brave and bold.
Rustling leaves, a gentle sigh,
As nature breathes a lullaby.

Mossy carpets cradle feet,
In harmony, the world we greet.
Trees stand tall with stories shared,
Guardians of secrets long declared.

Each footfall sings a timeless tune,
Beneath the watchful eye of moon.
Where light and shadow intertwine,
In this sanctuary, we align.

Listen close, the forest speaks,
In its embrace, our spirit seeks.
With every echo, we are free,
In the woods, we find the key.

The Poetry of Nightfall in Nature's Heart

As dusk descends, the sky ignites,
With shades of pink and purple flights.
The world embraces the dewy night,
In nature's heart, a pure delight.

Trees murmur soft, their leaves a song,
Where shadows dance, we all belong.
Crickets chirp their rhythmic beat,
While stars blend with the scents so sweet.

Nightfall weaves its tender threads,
In quiet moments, the heart spreads.
A gentle breeze whispers low,
Carrying dreams where rivers flow.

In the hush, our worries cease,
Wrapped in nature's warm embrace.
The essence of calm fills the air,
In the poetry we all share.

With every heartbeat, beauty glows,
Nightfall captures us, and flows.
Listen close as nature sighs,
Underneath the vast, starry skies.

Glowing Threads in the Green

In the forest's gentle breath,
Dancing lights weave through the trees,
Soft whispers of the earth's own heart,
Painting dreams upon the leaves.

Fireflies flicker, bright and bold,
Kaleidoscopes in dusk's warm hand,
Nature's art, a story told,
Each glowing thread, a magic strand.

Mossy carpets, emerald hue,
Woven paths of evening's grace,
Among the ferns, secrets lie,
In the stillness, time finds its place.

Branches arch like wise old hands,
Offering peace to wanderers' souls,
In this sanctuary of green,
The world outside slowly unfolds.

As stars peek through a velvet sky,
The forest hums a lullaby,
Glowing threads in the greenwood glade,
In quiet reverie, dreams are made.

Whirlwinds of Night and Nature

Whirling winds through silent trees,
Nature's breath, a solemn song,
Moonlit shadows weave and tease,
In the night where dreams belong.

Stars above in celestial dance,
Tell their tales of ages past,
Galaxies spin in wild romance,
While whispers echo, soft and fast.

Branches sway, an age-old rhythm,
In the heart of the night's embrace,
Every rustle, a silent hymn,
Nature's voice in sacred space.

Clouds drift by, like thoughts set free,
Shaping images unknown,
In whispers shared between the trees,
Each moment feels like home.

Beneath the sky, so deep and wide,
The whirlwinds spin in gentle flight,
Where night and nature lovingly collide,
In a boundless tapestry of light.

Mysteries of the Twinkling Grove

In the grove where shadows play,
Mysteries hide beneath the boughs,
Each rustling leaf has tales to say,
Of ancient times and solemn vows.

Twinkling lights like secrets shared,
Guide the wanderers through the night,
Illuminating paths once dared,
Beneath the stars, dreams take flight.

The air, alive with whispers fine,
Stirs the heart with stories old,
In every breeze, signs intertwine,
Nature's magic, boundless, bold.

Beneath the arch of a silver moon,
The grove unveils its timeless lore,
Swaying gently to a haunting tune,
An invitation to explore.

In every corner, wonder nested,
Each moment, a new intrigue,
The mysteries of the grove rested,
In twinkling stars, our hearts fatigue.

Silent Watchers of the Midnight Sky

Above the world, in tranquil grace,
Stars like sentinels stand high,
Silent watchers of the night's embrace,
Guardians in the vast, deep sky.

Their glimmers whisper of time's flow,
Chasing shadows that softly sway,
In the stillness, secrets grow,
The dance of night leads dreams astray.

Beneath their gaze, the earth finds peace,
Wrapped in twilight's calming shroud,
A moment's pause, a sweet release,
As the heavens wear a jeweled crown.

Clouds drift lazily, softly charting,
Paths of wonder; the world below,
In silence, hearts begin their parting,
With hopes that in starlight flow.

In this celestial night, we ponder,
What lies beyond each twinkling ray,
As the silent watchers leave us to wander,
In the depths of dreams until the day.

Secrets Whispered in Moonbeams

In the stillness of night,
Whispers trace the air's sighs.
Softly glowing silver light,
Secrets wander where time flies.

Beneath the ancient trees,
Dreams entwined with twinkling stars.
Echoes of forgotten pleas,
Carried high in quiet bars.

Moonlit paths of mystery,
Dancing shadows softly blend.
Each heart holds a history,
Stories where the lost descend.

Gentle breezes touch the ground,
A lullaby of silent hopes.
In the silence, truths are found,
As the night, in peace, elopes.

Secrets, woven in the dark,
Tales etched in the silver beams.
With every flicker, a spark,
Illuminates our timid dreams.

A Voyage Through Celestial Branches

Stars adorn the cosmic sea,
Branches reach for realms unknown.
Guided by the night's decree,
Time slips by, forever flown.

Galaxies twirl in delight,
Fleeting echoes, whispers call.
Journey through the endless night,
Foundations built on stardust fall.

Winds of time sweep through the air,
Carrying tales of the vast.
Each moment captures a prayer,
Linking futures with the past.

A tapestry of endless dreams,
Woven through with light and sound.
In the heart, the wonder gleams,
As our souls in silence bound.

Voyagers of hidden skies,
Charting paths where shadows dwell.
In the stars, our spirit flies,
On celestial branches swell.

Twilight's Canvas Over Mossy Beds

In twilight's soft embrace,
Colors dance on shadows' glide.
Nature paints with gentle grace,
On mossy beds, where dreams reside.

Shimmers of the day retreat,
Veils of dusk begin to weave.
Every heartbeat feels the beat,
In a realm where time believes.

Silhouettes of trees arise,
Framing whispers in the night.
Underneath the starlit skies,
Sleepy creatures share their plight.

Moonlight drapes like silken cloth,
Covering the woodland floor.
In the calm, we find a troth,
Nature's art forevermore.

A canvas draped in twilight hue,
Memories etched in silent breaths.
In this stillness, we renew,
Settling in with love's caress.

The Melodies of Shadows and Stars

In the quiet, whispers play,
Melodies drift through the air.
Shadows dance in night's ballet,
Composing dreams with gentle care.

Stars above in soft array,
Echoes of a world complete.
In the dark, our hearts convey,
Tender tales in rhythmic beat.

Harmony of light and shade,
Blending notes of silent grace.
In this symphony, we wade,
Finding solace in the space.

Timeless songs of night unfold,
As the universe aligns.
In our spirits, truth behold,
As the music softly shines.

Together, we'll embrace the art,
Of shadows twirling with the light.
In the night, we'll find our heart,
Woven deep in sounds of night.

Twilight's Embrace on Tall Trees

The sun dips low, the sky ignites,
Shadows stretch in fading light.
Whispers dance on gentle leaves,
Nature sighs, as day now grieves.

Branches cradle, holding time,
A canvas of the night sublime.
Stars awake with crisp delight,
In twilight's embrace, all feels right.

The forest hums a soft refrain,
With every breath, a sweet refrain.
Moonlight spills like silken threads,
Weaving dreams where silence spreads.

A hush descends, the world subsides,
Softly drifting, all confides.
In this moment, hearts entwine,
Bound by dusk's ephemeral line.

Whispers of the evening call,
In this realm, we find it all.
Between the branches, beauty flows,
Twilight's love, the heart still knows.

A Glimpse of Stars Through Foliage

Amidst the leaves, a secret sight,
Glimmering gems, the endless night.
Silver whispers through the trees,
A cosmic glance, a gentle breeze.

Dappled light on forest floor,
Each twinkling spark, we long to adore.
The canopy, a tapestry wide,
Hides a universe, where dreams abide.

Notes of crickets serenade,
As moonbeams dance in twilight's glade.
A moment caught in nature's grace,
Every star finds its rightful place.

Branches sway, a lullaby sweet,
With every pulse, the heart can beat.
So close, the night, the stars so bright,
Whispering tales in soft moonlight.

Through every leaf, a story spun,
A glimpse of magic, each and every one.
In stillness found, our wishes soar,
Stars through foliage forevermore.

Nocturnal Serenade Among the Boughs

Underneath the starry dome,
Crickets chirp, the woods a home.
In shadows deep, the night unfolds,
A serenade, where nature holds.

Gentle rustle, branches sway,
Whispers float, inviting play.
The moon takes stage, a radiant queen,
In nocturnal dreams, the air is keen.

Beneath the boughs, where silence rests,
Every heartbeat, the forest tests.
Notes collide in a sweet embrace,
As owls hoot in their secret space.

A lull of night, so deep, so wide,
In furry arms, the creatures hide.
Stars alight in silent cheer,
Filling hearts that dare to hear.

With every breeze, the night ignites,
A serenade from earthly heights.
In shadows' play, life's song prevails,
Among the boughs, the heart resides.

Cosmic Dance Over Alpine Heights

Above the peaks, where eagles fly,
Celestial rhythm meets the sky.
The stars twirl in a grand ballet,
While mountains watch, they sway all day.

Silver threads of starlit beams,
Bathed in dreams, the world redeems.
In the chill of night's embrace,
Nature sings at cosmic pace.

Majestic heights, bathed in light,
Echoes of the day take flight.
Galaxies spin in timeless grace,
While we stand in this sacred space.

With every breath, the universe breathes,
A wondrous dance, as heart believes.
Among the summits, where spirits rise,
We find our place beneath the skies.

In the stillness, whispers call,
The cosmic dance enchants us all.
Over alpine heights, we take our stand,
Together in this starry land.

Sighs of the Night in the Timbered Paths

Whispers rustle through the trees,
Echoes of a soft, cool breeze.
Moonlight dances on the ground,
Lost in peace, no other sound.

Branches sway, a gentle tune,
Stars peek through, a silver boon.
Nature's sighs, a calming balm,
Wrapped in night, the world is calm.

Footsteps soft on leaf-strewn trails,
A secret where the heart unveils.
As shadows stretch and fade away,
The magic of the night will stay.

Through the woods, a path so clear,
In every rustle, joy and fear.
A symphony of night unfolds,
Embracing stories yet untold.

The night, a cloak of dreams and sighs,
Enfolding all beneath its skies.
Timbered paths will guide the soul,
Through whispers, you'll become the whole.

Stargazing Through Nature's Boughs

Underneath a canopy,
Where stars peek through with melody.
Nature offers a grand display,
While crickets sing the night away.

Branches swaying in the glow,
A tranquil magic starts to flow.
Constellations tell their tales,
As moonlight slips through leafy veils.

In this peaceful, sacred space,
The universe shows its face.
Every twinkle a soft embrace,
In this vastness, we find our place.

As shooting stars race through the night,
Each wish made feels just so right.
Underneath this cosmic dome,
In nature's arms, we feel at home.

The boughs hold secrets, old and wise,
While dreams unfold beneath the skies.
A moment caught in timeless flow,
We watch the night, the heart aglow.

A Tapestry Woven by Nightfall

Threads of silver gently spun,
With every dusk, the day is done.
Nightfall speaks in whispers low,
Painting shadows, soft and slow.

Stars are stitches in the dark,
Illuminating every spark.
Nature's loom awaits the dawn,
As we breathe a dream reborn.

With each moment, night will weave,
Stories that we can't believe.
Mysteries wrapped in gentle night,
Darkness transformed by soft moonlight.

Every breeze a subtle thread,
Weaving paths in which we tread.
A tapestry both grand and small,
In every heart, a nightfall call.

Tales of wonder interlace,
Under the stars' warm, soft embrace.
In night's fabric, we find delight,
A masterpiece of love and light.

Dreaming in the Embrace of Pines

Beneath the pines, a world so still,
Where shadows lie and dreams fulfill.
The scent of earth is sweet and deep,
In the forest's heart, we quietly seep.

Whispers of the wind call clear,
In this haven, there's no fear.
Each breath a rhythm, soft and low,
As nature cradles us in flow.

Stars peek through the branches high,
While nightingale sings lullabies.
In these woods, we gently sway,
Gathering dreams along the way.

Underneath the watchful gaze,
Wrapped in warmth, our spirits blaze.
Every sigh, a note of peace,
In pines' embrace, our worries cease.

With every heartbeat, nature's hymn,
In the twilight, we swim within.
Together, lost in dreams divine,
We find ourselves, where hearts entwine.

Eclipsed Echoes in the Wilderness

Whispers dance through the trees,
Moonlight kisses the brook's ease,
Shadows stretch and fade away,
Nature holds its breath to stay.

Echoes linger, soft and low,
Secrets carried by the flow,
Stars above in silent grace,
Embrace night's tender face.

Branches sway in hush and sigh,
While the night begins to cry,
Memories are lost in dreams,
Wilderness glows in moonbeams.

Footprints left on paths untraced,
Beauty in each step embraced,
Through the dark, a journey vast,
Eclipsed echoes from the past.

In the wild, we seek to find,
Nature's heart, so intertwined,
Every sound, a tale untold,
In the wilderness, bold and old.

Luminous Visions Beyond the Branches

In the dawn, a golden hue,
Through the leaves, the sky breaks blue,
Whispers of a brand new day,
Luminous visions lead the way.

Sunlight dances on the ground,
Nature's beauty all around,
Branch by branch, the light unfolds,
Secrets of the forest told.

Birds take flight, a joyful song,
In this place where dreams belong,
Beyond the branches, hopes arise,
Touch the soft and endless skies.

With each step, the heart ignites,
Wonders bloom in morning's sights,
Every leaf a tale to share,
Luminous visions in the air.

As we wander, time stands still,
Nature's whispers gently thrill,
Boundless dreams in sunlight dance,
In this realm of sweet romance.

The Serenity of Nebula-kissed Limbs

Under stars that softly gleam,
Branches sway in cosmic dream,
Nebula kisses every leaf,
In this space, we find relief.

Moonlight drapes the world in peace,
Nature's whispers never cease,
Every limb a sacred song,
In the night, we all belong.

Celestial sights fill the sky,
In this hush, we learn to fly,
Every shadow, beauty wakes,
In the stillness, the heart aches.

Stars align in patterns bright,
Guiding us to endless light,
Serenity, a sweet embrace,
In the wilderness, find your place.

Among the trees, we seek our dreams,
Underneath the cosmic beams,
Linked by night, we breathe as one,
Nebula-kissed, our journey's begun.

Night's Embrace on Silent Trails

On silent trails where shadows play,
Night unfolds, guiding our way,
Whispers of the moonlit air,
In this peace, we shed our care.

Paths of silver, soft and still,
Every breath, a gentle thrill,
Nature wrapped in twilight's hug,
Under stars, our spirits shrug.

Crickets sing their serenade,
As the forest's song won't fade,
In this moment, time stands tall,
Night's embrace forever calls.

With each step, the heartbeats blend,
In this magic, joys transcend,
Silent trails, a journey long,
Wrapped in night, we find our song.

In the dark, the world feels wide,
With the moon as our guide,
Together in this sacred space,
In night's embrace, we find our place.

Glimmers Through Leafy Veils

Sunlight dances through the trees,
Casting gold on gentle leaves.
Whispers float upon the breeze,
Nature's song, the heart believes.

Dappled light in quiet glades,
Secrets held in emerald waves.
Life awakens as it fades,
In the shade, the spirit braves.

Shadows play, a shifting scene,
Branches sway, a vibrant quilt.
In this space, we find the serene,
A world of wonder gently built.

Rippling streams with laughter flow,
Mirrored skies in tranquil pools.
Here, the heart begins to glow,
Amidst the whispers of nature's rules.

Glimmers shine where hopes reside,
Hidden dreams begin to unveil.
In leafy veils, our hearts confide,
A journey begins in nature's tale.

Serenade of the Nightfall Shadows

As twilight sets, the stars arise,
A blanket dark, where silence hums.
Moonlit paths and whispered sighs,
The night in its embrace becomes.

Shadows dance on silver beams,
Softly weaving tales untold.
In the darkness, magic gleams,
Embracing dreams with hearts behold.

Beneath the sky, a stillness reigns,
Nightfall sings in soothing tones.
Echoes floating through the plains,
A symphony of gentle moans.

In whispers low, the crickets play,
A serenade to stars alive.
Nature's nocturne on display,
Where all the wandering souls arrive.

Moments linger, time unwinds,
In shadows, mysteries unfurl.
The night bequeaths what it finds,
A melody in twilight's swirl.

Celestial Echoes in the Wilderness

In the heights where eagles soar,
Celestial whispers intertwine.
Forest depths that lovers explore,
Nature sings in rhythm divine.

Mountains rise to touch the stars,
Guardians of the ancient earth.
Echoes drift from distant afar,
Each note a testament of worth.

Amidst the leaves, a heartbeat strong,
The wilderness in harmony thrives.
Every creature, every song,
A tapestry where life survives.

In golden rays of dawn's embrace,
The wild awakens, fresh and bright.
Nature's beauty, time can't erase,
Celestial echoes greet the light.

And as the world begins to turn,
Our hearts awaken to its call.
In wilderness, a spark will burn,
Echoes linger, binding all.

Radiance Between the Branches

In the canopy, light finds its way,
A glow that brushes tender leaves.
Morning breaks with golden ray,
In each beam, the soul believes.

Branches weave their silent tales,
Fragrant blooms in colors bright.
Nature's story, the heart exhales,
In this haven, pure delight.

Beneath the boughs, the dreams take flight,
Sunlit pathways, shadows play.
Here in stillness, all feels right,
Where peace and wonder softly sway.

Radiant whispers in the air,
As butterflies begin to twirl.
Life's embrace in moments rare,
In freedom's dance, the heart unfurls.

Between the branches, magic glows,
A world alive, forever new.
In every moment, joy bestows,
Radiance shared in every view.

The Music of Cosmic Shadows

Stars weave a tune in the night,
Whispers of tales, taking flight.
Galaxies dance in cosmic embrace,
Time slows down in this vast space.

Notes ripple soft through the void,
Echoing dreams once deployed.
If silence reveals the heart's call,
In shadows, we find it all.

Celestial symphonies rise,
Melding the dark, the bright skies.
In the stillness, we hear the sound,
Of mystery swirling all around.

Each note a thread in the weave,
Of universes we dare believe.
Brought forth by starlight's warm glow,
In cosmic shadows, secrets flow.

With every chord, we become whole,
Finding harmony in the soul.
For in this night, we are bound,
In music, the cosmic is found.

Starlight on the Forest Floor

Moonlight dapples the ground,
Starlit secrets all around.
Whispers of leaves, soft and low,
Embracing night, gentle glow.

Beneath the canopy of dreams,
A silver glint, the world gleams.
Nature's breath in calming sighs,
As twinkling gems light the skies.

Cool shadows mold the night air,
Filling our hearts with deep care.
The rustle of branches above,
Wraps us in nature's pure love.

Soft footfalls on mossy trails,
In the night, the magic sails.
Every step a story untold,
In the beauty, we find gold.

Together we walk, hand in hand,
Starlit path through all the land.
In the forest's quiet restore,
We find our peace, forevermore.

Embracing the Night in Wooded Refuge

In the wood, where shadows blend,
The night unfolds, a trust to send.
Nestled deep in twilight's arms,
Nature's embrace, it warm disarms.

Stars peep through the boughs above,
Whispering tales of peace and love.
In the quiet, our spirits soar,
In the dark, we find what's more.

The cool air carries a song,
Echoes of where we belong.
With each breeze, a heartbeat shared,
In this refuge, all is cared.

Moss and ferns cushion our stay,
As night unfolds, the light fades away.
We breathe in the earth's playful tune,
As hearts align with the silver moon.

Wrapped in the night, we remain,
In wooded refuge, joy and pain.
Together we sway to the sound,
Of whispers in shadows, love profound.

Flickers of Brilliance Through the Dark

In the deep of night, sparks ignite,
Flickers of hope, burning bright.
Each star a promise woven anew,
Guiding the lost, the seekers too.

Through the veil, light starts to show,
Blazing trails where dreams will flow.
In the dark, a dance takes shape,
Of shimmering wishes, no escape.

Whispers of fate guide the way,
As shadows shift and gently play.
In every flicker, courage calls,
Lifting our spirits as night falls.

Dancing with light, we break free,
Embracing the dark, we learn to see.
With every spark, the heart ignites,
Creating magic in starry nights.

In twilight's grasp, the brilliance shines,
Beneath the weight of ancient pines.
Emboldened by dreams, forever embark,
Chasing the flickers that light the dark.

The Night's Breath Among Spruce and Fir

The moonlight bathes the trees,
Whispers dance in the dark breeze.
Silent shadows weave and twine,
In this peaceful world, divine.

Stars peek through the emerald veil,
Soft secrets ride the gentle gale.
Pine scents linger in the air,
Nature's quiet song everywhere.

Owls hoot, a distant call,
Night's embrace enfolds us all.
Crickets chirp in rhythmic praise,
Life unfolds in tender ways.

Mist wraps round the trunk so tight,
Veiling dreams in silver light.
The world is hushed, a slumber deep,
In spruce and fir, our thoughts we keep.

Lost in time, the heart aligns,
Beneath the sky, where magic shines.
In the night's breath, we take flight,
Spruce and fir, our spirits' light.

Reveries in a Forest of Glow

Sunset paints the sky with fire,
Nature's colors never tire.
Beneath the branches, shadows play,
As night yields to the end of day.

Glow worms flicker, soft and shy,
Lighting paths beneath the sky.
In this forest, dreams take flight,
With every whispered word of night.

The air is charged, a gentle hum,
Memories of summer come.
Leaves rustle like a soothing song,
In this haven, we belong.

Stars awaken, one by one,
Guiding hearts until we're done.
In these reveries, we explore,
A universe behind the door.

Time stands still, we lose the race,
In this dream-like, sacred space.
Among the trees, our spirits flow,
In the forest's warm, soft glow.

Guiding Lights Beyond the Wilderness

A beacon shines in the wild night,
Whispers of hope in fading light.
Through dense thickets, shadows loom,
Yet stars above promise bloom.

Footsteps echo on the ground,
In this wilderness, peace is found.
The path winds softly through the trees,
A symphony of rustling leaves.

Guiding lights twinkle and gleam,
Floating softly, feel the dream.
Each flicker holds a tale untold,
Of journeys brave, of hearts bold.

The compass spins, the heart knows true,
In wild terrain, we must pursue.
As darkness deepens, friendships grow,
An endless stream of warm, sweet glow.

Beyond the trees, the moon does cast,
Its silvery light is unsurpassed.
Together, we walk hand in hand,
In this wilderness, a promised land.

Enigma of the Cosmic Canopy

Above us spins a wondrous sight,
The cosmic dance, a tapestry bright.
In the silence, secrets lie,
Stars like diamonds in the sky.

A canopy of dreams unfolds,
Tales of ages, stories told.
Winds whisper through the ancient boughs,
While starlight deepens nature's vows.

Recorded in the heart of night,
Mysteries twinkle, hearts take flight.
Every shimmer, a wish anew,
In this enigma, visions grew.

Beneath this vast and open dome,
In the universe, we find our home.
Galaxies twirl, a swirling spree,
In the cosmos, feel the glee.

So when you gaze at heaven's art,
Know the universe calls the heart.
In the canopy where dreams entwine,
We are cosmic threads, divine.

Transcendence Through a Starry Lens

In the velvet sky, dreams unfold,
Countless stories in starlight told.
Wonders shimmer from afar,
Guiding hearts, our bright North Star.

Wisps of cosmos, gently weave,
Infinite truths, we dare believe.
Visions painted in heavenly hues,
Whispers of ancient cosmic views.

A bridge of light, across the night,
Connecting souls, igniting light.
Through the void, our spirits soar,
Transcendence calls, forevermore.

Galaxies spin, in rhythmic dance,
In this vastness, we find our chance.
Merging with the astral sea,
In boundless love, we come to be.

Every twinkle, a soft embrace,
Interwoven in time and space.
Underneath this endless dome,
In starlit dreams, we find our home.

The Embrace of Night Among Timber Spirits

Beneath the boughs, secrets reside,
Where timber spirits gently guide.
Whispers echo through the trees,
Carried softly on the breeze.

Moonlight bathes the forest floor,
Mysteries beckon, forevermore.
In shadows deep, the wild things play,
As night unfolds, they come to stay.

Each rustling leaf, a tale to tell,
In twilight's hush, enchantments swell.
The air is thick with dreams unspoken,
In timeless realms, hearts are woken.

Embrace the dark, for it's alive,
Among the pines, our spirits thrive.
In unity with nature's song,
We find the place where we belong.

As the night wraps us in its cloak,
Timber spirits softly evoke.
In shadows deep, our fears take flight,
In the embrace of the serene night.

Ethereal Glow in the Whispering Pines

In the whispering pines, a glow appears,
Softly lighting the path for years.
An ethereal touch caresses the night,
Illuminating dreams with gentle light.

Beneath the branches, a stillness grows,
In nature's heart, a magic flows.
The air is rich with fragrant balm,
Wrapped in peace, our souls are calm.

Dancing shadows, flicker and fade,
In this realm, enchantments are laid.
Every moment, a treasure to keep,
In the glowing pines, secrets deep.

Stars pierce the canopy, shimmering bright,
Filling the world with pure delight.
With each rustle, the forest sings,
A serenade of wondrous things.

The glow beckons, inviting embrace,
A haven found in this sacred space.
Underneath this celestial dome,
In whispered dreams, we feel at home.

Shadows Dancing in Celestial Light

In heavenly realms, shadows sway,
Dancing lightly, they come to play.
Beneath the stars, a beautiful sight,
Whirling in rhythm, full of light.

Eclipsed in grace, they weave and twine,
A ballet spun on the edge of time.
Each twist and turn, a story unfolds,
In cosmic embrace, the universe holds.

Echoes of laughter, soft and sweet,
In this celestial dance, we meet.
Every heartbeat, a cosmic tune,
Resonating under the watchful moon.

Shadows cradle all that we are,
Illuminating dreams from afar.
In their embrace, we find delight,
Lost in the magic of celestial light.

Hand in hand, we float and glide,
In this party of stars, we abide.
With shadows as guides, we take flight,
And dance forever in endless night.

Whispers of the Night Canopy

In the hush of twilight's grace,
Leaves murmur secrets through the space.
Stars twinkle with a gentle sigh,
As shadows dance and softly lie.

Crickets sing in rhythmic tune,
Under the watchful, silver moon.
The forest breathes a soothing sound,
Where hidden dreams and truths abound.

Among the branches, silence weaves,
A tapestry where wonder breathes.
Each rustling leaf, a whispered prayer,
Entwined with hope that lingers there.

Owls glide softly through the dark,
Witnessing the night's sweet spark.
Mysteries weave through ancient trees,
In every sigh, a gentle tease.

So close your eyes and take a flight,
Upon the whispers of the night.
Let the canopy cradle your dreams,
In a world where nothing's as it seems.

Dreams Amidst the Evergreen

Beneath the boughs of emerald pride,
Where secrets of the forest hide.
The air infused with pine's embrace,
Invites us to this sacred space.

Amidst the roots where shadows play,
Lies a world that dreams away.
Gentle breezes shift and sway,
Carrying thoughts of yesterday.

Ferns whisper tales from ages past,
In every breeze, a spell is cast.
Stars peek through the leafy veil,
While crickets weave their nightly tale.

A moonbeam's touch on mossy ground,
Awakens dreams in silence found.
Every heartbeat intertwined,
With the magic of nature aligned.

So linger here, let worries cease,
In this realm of tranquil peace.
For in the green, our spirits roam,
Finding solace, finding home.

Celestial Shadows in the Woods

In the woods where shadows dwell,
Stars above weave secret spells.
Moonlit paths that twist and turn,
Guiding souls with fire's burn.

Each step echoes through the night,
Wrapped in the cosmos' light.
Branches stretch like fingers wide,
Inviting dreams, no need to hide.

Soft whispers linger in the air,
Crafting magic everywhere.
Celestial bodies softly gleam,
Waking hearts from quiet dream.

Night unfolds its velvet cloak,
With each breath, a story spoke.
In shadows deep, the mysteries lie,
Where fate and wonder softly sigh.

So dance within this starry maze,
And let your spirit find its ways.
In cosmic shadows, find your song,
Where every heart can feel they belong.

Moonlit Forest Secrets

Beneath the glow of silver light,
The forest pulses, warm and bright.
Hidden paths and stories old,
Unfold in whispers, brave and bold.

Moonbeams guide the quiet feet,
Where nature's tales and shadows meet.
Each rustling leaf a secret kept,
In every nook, the wild has leapt.

Fairy lights in twinkling dance,
Invite the heart to take a chance.
The sigh of trees, a gentle balm,
Filling night's embrace with calm.

Softly now, the world feels right,
Wrapped within the arms of night.
In moonlit charm, let worries cease,
And taste the magic, feel the peace.

Each secret held in nature's fold,
A treasure trove of stories told.
In this forest, find your place,
As moonlit shadows leave a trace.

Glimmering Dreams in the Gnarled Arms

In twilight's hush, where shadows blend,
A whisper of wishes, quiet and free.
Gnarled branches cradle the dreams we send,
In the heart of the woods, there's magic to see.

Each star a story, softly it gleams,
Threads of silver weave through the night.
In this stillness, we gather our dreams,
Hoping to find each lost guiding light.

The cool breeze carries a secret song,
Nature's embrace wraps us within.
In these dark depths, we feel we belong,
Awaking the calm that lives deep within.

With every heartbeat, the world drifts away,
Presence of wonder fills the silent air.
In the gnarled arms where the shadows play,
Glimmering dreams weave patterns so rare.

The night unfolds, painting paths anew,
In the twilight hour, we softly tread.
In the embrace of the old and the true,
Our glimmering dreams guide where we're led.

Starlight's Kiss on Needle-tipped Leaves

Under the moon, where soft shadows dance,
Starlight kisses the needle-tipped leaves.
A carpet of emerald, a dreamy expanse,
Whispers of twilight, as the heart believes.

Silver droplets hang in delicate grace,
Nature's artistry, pure and divine.
Each leaf a canvas of time and space,
Catching the shimmer where darkness aligns.

In shadows they shimmer, secrets unfold,
Stories of starlight left here as a trace.
The night embraces the bold and the old,
A gentle reminder of love's warm embrace.

Through forests enchanted, our spirits will roam,
Dancing with dreams, we are solemnly stirred.
In this sacred haven, our hearts find a home,
As starlight's kiss speaks what words have deferred.

The soft rustle hums a sweet serenade,
A lullaby woven with nature's deep breath.
In the stillness of night, all worry will fade,
Find joy in the starlight, defying all death.

The Mystery Beneath the Night Sky

Under the vastness, questions arise,
The night sky holds secrets not easily seen.
Stars whisper tales to the moon's gentle sighs,
Inviting the curious, both simple and keen.

In shadows we wander, our thoughts in a whirl,
Each twinkle a promise, a beacon of hope.
The universe beckons, its wonders unfurl,
Like dreams that encourage our hearts to cope.

What lies in the dark, beneath the starlight?
Mysteries linger in the cool night air.
We trace the constellations, hearts burning bright,
Longing for answers, a glimpse to lay bare.

As dawn starts to break, we'll carry the light,
Woven with stardust, our souls intertwine.
In the throes of the evening, there's magic in sight,
With each glowing moment, the universe shines.

So, let us embrace what the night has to share,
In the depths of the dark, find courage and glee.
The mystery beckons, with love we declare,
In the vastness of night, together we're free.

Illuminated Pathways in Darkened Woods

Through darkened woods, where shadows entwine,
Sunlight trickles down, a gentle caress.
Illuminated pathways begin to align,
Leading us forth with a sense of finesse.

Branches sway softly, a lullaby's tune,
An invitation to dance in the shade.
Underneath canopies, dreams are attuned,
In nature's embrace, our worries will fade.

The golden light flickers, a spark in the trees,
Guiding our hearts with a warm, gentle glow.
Whispers of magic blow soft in the breeze,
Promises glisten where secrets may flow.

Together we wander through ferns and tall grass,
Each step a reminder of journeys we share.
In the heart of the woods, fears quietly pass,
A tapestry woven with love in the air.

So let us get lost in this stunning embrace,
Where illuminated pathways weave round our souls.
In the darkened woods, we all find our place,
As nature awakens, our spirits are whole.

Starbound Whispers Beneath the Canopy

In the twilight's gentle glow,
Whispers rise from earth below.
Stars align in silent grace,
Casting dreams in soft embrace.

Leaves quiver as secrets weave,
Nature's heart begins to cleave.
Voices murmur through the night,
Guiding lost souls to the light.

The moonlight dances on the ground,
Echoes of the world profound.
In this realm where shadows play,
Mysteries bloom, night turns to day.

Branches sway, a lullaby,
As constellations paint the sky.
Every rustle tells a tale,
With the night winds in full sail.

Take my hand, let's drift away,
Through the dreams that trees convey.
Underneath this canopy,
We'll find all that we can be.

Forest Guardian Under a Starry Veil

Beneath the cloak of starlit sky,
The forest breathes a whispered sigh.
Ancient trees stand strong and still,
Guardians of the quiet hill.

Fireflies flicker in warm embrace,
Lighting paths through time and space.
Each shadow holds a secret tight,
In the depths of velvet night.

A symphony of rustling leaves,
A tale that only twilight weaves.
In this world where echoes blend,
Nature's voice will never end.

The guardian speaks through softest breeze,
Awakening our souls with ease.
Underneath this vast expanse,
We are pulled into the dance.

With every step, our hearts align,
In harmony, a love divine.
Under this starry, whispering veil,
Together, we shall surely sail.

Celestial Canopy of Flickering Light

Above, a tapestry unfolds,
A celestial dream of stories told.
Stars in motion, twinkling bright,
A canopy of pure delight.

Winds carry songs from far away,
Brushing through as night meets day.
Each flicker hints at secrets bare,
Holding magic in the air.

With every rustle, shadows dance,
In moon's soft glow, we take a chance.
Guided by the glow we see,
Each moment whispers 'you and me.'

The night unveils its shimmering heart,
Bonding dreams that shall not part.
In this realm of boundless flight,
We'll weave our paths like starlit light.

Swaying branches bend with grace,
As we navigate this sacred space.
Underneath the sky so vast,
Each fleeting moment is a blast.

Enigma in the Starlit Thicket

Hidden deep within the woods,
A mystery the night concludes.
In starlit thickets, silence reigns,
Where each heartbeat softly remains.

Paths entwine through shadows cast,
Ghostly whispers of the past.
Crickets serenade the night,
With melodies both dark and light.

Patterns painted by the moon,
Echoes of a whispered tune.
Nature breathes a gentle sigh,
As starlight lingers low and high.

Here the enigma unfolds wide,
Beneath the sky, our hopes confide.
In each rustle, stories grow,
The magic of the night will flow.

With courage in our hearts so bright,
We'll unravel the veils of night.
Each discovery, a fragrant bloom,
In this thicket, there is room.

Timbered Paths Under Moonlit Skies

Whispers float on the gentle breeze,
As shadows dance beneath the trees.
Moonlit paths weave in and out,
Guiding hearts with serene doubt.

Branches sway with a soft embrace,
Each step taken, a quiet grace.
Stars above twinkle, bold and bright,
Lighting dreams on this tranquil night.

The night air cool, the world at rest,
In this moment, we feel so blessed.
Timbered wonders call us near,
Their ancient secrets whispering clear.

In the stillness, shadows play,
Nature's song, a sweet ballet.
Echoes linger, softly swell,
Among the trees where spirits dwell.

With every step, the night unfolds,
Stories of life in whispers told.
Together here beneath the stars,
Timbered paths will heal our scars.

A Celestial Journey Through the Pines

Underneath a canopy of green,
Pines stand tall, a sight serene.
Stars above begin to gleam,
Guided by a celestial dream.

The moon peeks through the branches high,
Painting silver on the sky.
Each breath taken, fresh and deep,
In pine-scented woods where secrets sleep.

Crisp night air whispers tales anew,
Of travelers lost, and paths they drew.
A journey through the trees unfolds,
With ancient wisdom in each hold.

Beneath the stars, our spirits soar,
Past skies painted with myth and lore.
The constellations light our way,
Through the pines, we find our stay.

In quiet moments, we reflect,
On journeys taken, and paths we select.
Amidst the pines, our hearts align,
In this celestial dance, divine.

Flickering Fireflies Through the Fir Trees

Flickering lights in the dusky haze,
Fireflies twirl in a joyful craze.
Among the firs, they weave their dance,
A magical moment, a fleeting chance.

Soft whispers echo in the night,
Nature's revelry, pure delight.
Each glow a spark of fleeting fire,
Lighting paths of sweet desire.

In shadows deep, they find their flight,
Guiding us through the starry night.
Among the firs, their winks collide,
A symphony of light where dreams abide.

Dancing breezes tease the trees,
As night unfolds with gentle ease.
Flickering lanterns in the dark,
Kindling hope with each bright spark.

The forest hums a soothing tune,
In the embrace of the silver moon.
Flickering lights enchant our eyes,
Through fir trees, our spirits rise.

Night's Melody Among the Conifers

A melody strums through the night,
Among conifers, hearts take flight.
Whispers carried on the wind,
Nature's anthem softly pinned.

The crisp air hums a gentle song,
As shadows lengthen, all night long.
Underneath the stars aglow,
The land reveals its inner flow.

Rustling leaves in harmony,
Echoes of wild symphony.
Each note a promise, pure and true,
Carried through the forest's view.

In this night, where dreams ignite,
Melodies linger, pure delight.
Among conifers, souls unite,
Spirits soaring into the night.

Voices of nature, soft and low,
Dance with the moon's celestial glow.
Night's melody, a tender gift,
Through the trees, our hearts uplift.

Luminescence Among Whispering Leaves

In the hush of twilight's grace,
The leaves dance with a subtle glow.
Light spills softly from their trace,
A secret few have come to know.

Whispers echo in the air,
Filling hearts with gentle peace.
Each moment wrapped in quiet care,
Where nature's magic finds release.

Glowing orbs twinkle on high,
Cascading down in soft arrays.
As shadows linger, time slips by,
Charmed by the evening's soft displays.

Swaying branches play a tune,
A lullaby of rustling sounds.
Embraced beneath the watchful moon,
Where every heartbeat love surrounds.

In the vessel of this night,
Soul and spirit intertwine.
Lost in dreams that take to flight,
Within the luminescent vine.

Stars Drifting Through the Tall Pines

The stars are scattered, glimmers bright,
They weave through pines with tender grace.
A canvas draped in velvet light,
Creating magic in this space.

With every breeze, the whispers flow,
Telling tales of ages past.
Secrets hidden where shadows grow,
Reflections caught in dreams so vast.

Beneath the boughs, we lay in awe,
Our hearts aligned with cosmic beams.
The universe's ancient law,
Links our spirits in woven dreams.

In this moment, time stands still,
Lost in wonder, we breathe deep.
As silence wraps the world, we feel,
The beauty of the night we keep.

So let the stars drift on their way,
Through towering pines, we find our place.
In the stillness, here we'll stay,
Embraced within the night's soft face.

Beneath a Canopy of Wonder

Beneath the leaves where sunlight spills,
Magic lingers in every beam.
Nature whispers, and silence fills,
The air with hints of softest dream.

Each petal glows in colors rare,
As creatures flit from here to there.
In secret nooks, we pause to share,
The stories held in gentle care.

The branches sway, a soothing song,
As light and shadow intertwine.
Where every heart feels it belongs,
Within this place, so pure, divine.

We breathe the scent of earth and dew,
In harmony with life around.
With every glance, our spirits grew,
United with the soil and ground.

So let us wander, hand in hand,
Through winding paths where wonders lie.
In every moment, rich and grand,
We find our joy beneath the sky.

The Enchanted Grove at Dusk

The sun dips low, the shadows creep,
In the grove, a hush descends.
Whispers of magic softly seep,
As day to night, the world transcends.

Here, every leaf holds tales untold,
Starlit secrets held in embrace.
The air grows cool, the colors bold,
In this enchanting, sacred space.

A twilight spell begins to weave,
A tapestry of dusk and light.
In every glance, we dare believe,
The wonder wrapped within the night.

So close your eyes and take a breath,
Feel the pulse of earth and sky.
In this grove, there's life and death,
A circle spun, where spirits fly.

Together in this gentle sway,
We find our solace, hope, and dreams.
As night unfolds, we lose our way,
Yet in the dark, the magic gleams.

Milton Keynes UK
Ingram Content Group UK Ltd.
UKHW010228111224
452348UK00011B/591